LOOK & FIND OUT

# Polar Animals

by Alice B. McGinty

Scholastic Inc.

# How do animals live at the Poles?

## Long, cold winters

Snow, ice, wind

Food is hard to find

# Musk ox

The musk ox keeps warm with two coats of fur! Each winter, the musk ox grows a new inner coat of woolly fur.

The musk ox has another coat that grows over the inner coat of fur. The outer coat is made of long hairs that reach all the way to the animal's feet. This outer coat blocks the cold and wind.

# Arctic hare

It's hard to find food in the snow.

The arctic hare digs under the snow for woody plants. It also eats berries and mosses. When lakes and rivers are frozen, the arctic hare eats snow to get water.

# Rock ptarmigan

Many animals that live at the poles are white, so they are hard to see in the snow.

The rock ptarmigan is brown in the summer. Each winter, its feathers turn pure white. The ptarmigan matches the snow so that animals that want to eat it can't see it.

# Polar bear

Polar bears can move in many ways. The fur on their feet protects them when they walk over ice and snow.

Their wide front paws help them swim in the ocean. Polar bears even slide down icy hills on their bellies!

# Emperor penguin

Polar animals need a place to stay warm. Some stay out of the wind by living under the snow. Some nest in rocks, sheltered by cliffs.

Emperor penguins keep one another warm. They huddle together during winter storms. They protect one another from wind and snow.

# Caribou

Some animals move to warmer weather when winter comes. This is called migration.

Each fall, huge herds of caribou, also known as reindeer, leave the cold Arctic for warmer lands. In the spring, they go back to their polar home.

# Find Out More

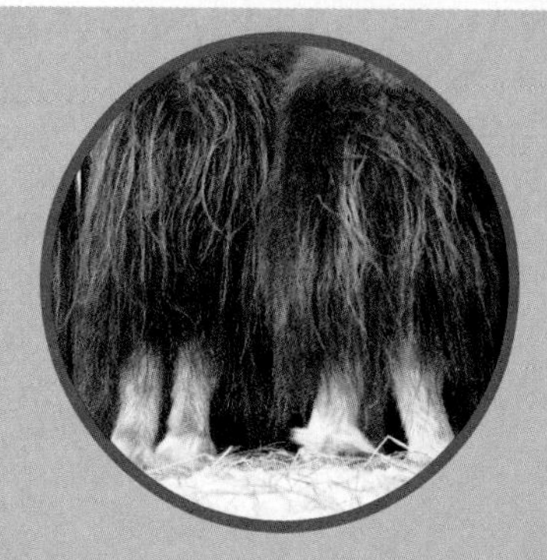

The musk ox's inner coat is eight times warmer than sheep's wool. The hollow hairs of the musk ox's outer coat hold in warmth and block wind.

The arctic hare has strong back legs. It can run fast, stand tall to reach food, and even hop while standing upright.

This black strip under the rock ptarmigan's eyes helps the bird see. The strip reduces the glare of the sun on the snow.

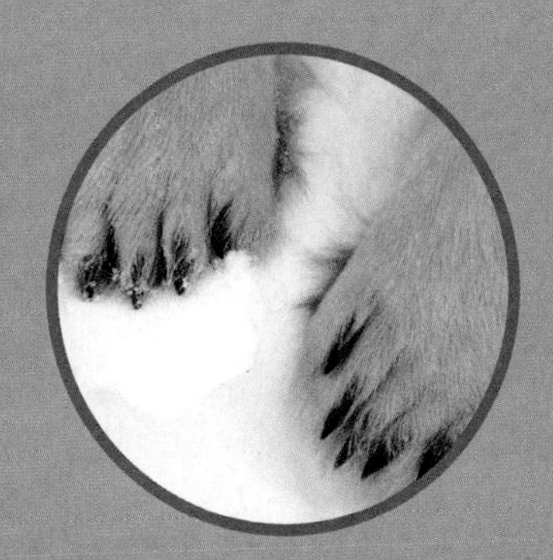

The polar bear's strong, sharp claws give it traction on slick ice, help it dig through snow, and are used to kill its prey.

Emperor penguin chicks stand on top of an adult's warm, padded feet. When the chick is older, it will stand on the cold ice by itself.

A caribou's wide hooves help it walk over miles of snow. The hooves are good for swimming, too.